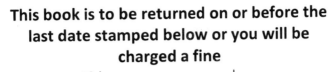

This book is to be returned on or before the last date stamped below or you will be charged a fine

New City College – Redbridge campus
Library and Learning Centre
Barley Lane
Romford RM6 4XT
https://towham.cirqahosting.com
Redbridge: 020 8548 7118

Adapted by: Jane Rollason
Publisher: Jacquie Bloese
Editor: Nicole Irving
Designer: Mo Choy
Picture research: Amparo Escobedo

Contents

Page

THE LITTLE PRINCE

is a boy. He lives on a very small planet. He asks many questions.

THE RED ROSE

comes to the Little Prince's planet.

THE FOX

is a clever animal. He understands the Little Prince.

THE KING

lives on a very small planet.

THE BUSINESSMAN
loves numbers.

THE MAN IN THE DESERT
flies planes.

PLACES

EARTH is our planet.

This DESERT is in Africa. It is very hot.

The Little Prince

CHAPTER 1
The red rose

The Little Prince lives on a very small planet. He has yellow hair and green clothes.

There is a problem on his planet. There are many baobab trees. Every day there are new baobab trees. The Little Prince wants to stop them. He works every day, but he can't stop them.

One day, a new tree arrives on the Little Prince's planet. The Little Prince watches it for five days.

On the sixth day, the new tree opens. But it isn't a tree. It's a rose!

'You are very beautiful,' the Little Prince says.

'Yes, I am beautiful,' the rose says. 'I am a red rose. I am the *only* red rose.'

The prince looks at the rose.

'Well?' the rose says. 'Isn't it time for breakfast?'

'Oh!' the Little Prince says. 'I'm sorry!'

He gives her some water. But the rose isn't happy.

The rose is never happy. Every day she has a new problem.

First, the planet is cold. Then it's hot.

So the prince is sad.

One day, the Little Prince says to the rose, 'I'm leaving.'
'Oh,' the rose says. Now *she* is sad.
'Aren't you angry with me?' the Little Prince asks.
'No, I'm not angry,' the rose says. 'I'm sorry. I'm a bad rose.'
The rose loves the Little Prince.
'Please be happy,' she says. 'Now, go!'
The Little Prince flies away.
And the rose cries.

CHAPTER 2
Two new planets

The Little Prince goes to some new planets.

On the first planet, he meets a king. The king is the only person on this planet.

'Every person on my planet listens to me,' the king says.
'But you're the only person here,' says the Little Prince.
'The people on planet Earth listen to me,' the king says.
'They can't hear you.'

'*You* can hear me,' says the king.
'But I'm going now,' the Little Prince says.
'Go!' says the king.
And the Little Prince flies away.
'You see!' the king says. '*You* are listening to me!'
'Grown-ups are strange,' the Little Prince thinks.

On the second planet, the Little Prince finds a businessman.

'I can't talk to you,' the businessman says. 'I haven't got time.'

'What are you doing?' the Little Prince asks.

'I'm counting my money,' the businessman says.

'Why?' the Little Prince asks.

'Because money is very important,' the businessman says.

'What can you do with your money?' the Little Prince asks.

'I can count it again!'

And the Little Prince flies away.

'Grown-ups are strange,' he thinks.

CHAPTER 3
Planet Earth

Earth is a big planet. It doesn't have one king and one businessman. It has 111 kings and 900,000 businessmen. It has seven billion people on it!

The Little Prince arrives on Earth. He doesn't see seven billion people. He doesn't see any people. Suddenly, he sees a blue light. It's going very fast. The light stops next to him. It isn't a blue light. It's a blue snake.

'Good evening,' the Little Prince says.

'Good evening,' the snake says.

'What planet is this?'

'This is Earth,' the snake answers.

'Where are the people?' the Little Prince asks.

'This is the desert. There are no people here,' the snake says. 'Earth is very big.'

The Little Prince looks up. 'Look at my planet,' he says to the snake.

'It's beautiful,' the snake says. 'So why are you here?'

'I have a problem with a rose,' the Little Prince says.

'Ah!' says the snake.

'You're strange,' the Little Prince says. 'You have no legs.'

'Men don't like me. They run away from me.'

'But you are very small,' the Little Prince says.

'I am very fast and very clever. I can help you. I can take you to your planet. Remember me!'

'I understand,' the Little Prince says. 'Goodbye.'

After many hours, the Little Prince comes to a house
in the desert. It has a garden. There are many red roses in
this garden.

'Hello,' the roses say.

The Little Prince doesn't smile. So his red rose is *not* the
only red rose.

'Where are the people?' the Little Prince thinks.

But the people are in the house. They are not thinking
about the roses.

Then a fox comes into the garden.

'Can you play with me?' the Little Prince asks. 'I'm very sad.'

'No,' the fox says. 'I'm not tame. And boys and foxes are not usually friends.'

'Please,' the Little Prince says.

They walk out of the garden to a tree.

'There are many boys on Earth,' the fox says. 'You are not different from them. You are not special to me.'

'How can I be special to you?' the Little Prince asks.

'You can tame me,' the fox says. 'Let's try. First, sit down here. Don't look at me. Don't talk.'

The Little Prince sits down. The fox sits five metres away and watches him.

'I'm going now,' says the fox after an hour. 'Come here to the tree at four o'clock tomorrow.'

The second day, the Little Prince comes to the tree. He comes at four o'clock. The fox is waiting and the Little Prince sits down.

The fox sits four metres away and watches him.

The third day, the fox sits three metres away.

The fourth day, the fox sits next to the Little Prince.

'There!' the fox says. 'Now we are friends. You are *my* boy. I see you and I am happy!'

Every day, they come to the tree at four o'clock.

'Now I understand,' the Little Prince says. 'You are my special fox. The red rose is my special rose. It is the same thing.'

One day, the Little Prince says to the fox, 'I'm leaving.
I'm going back to my rose.'

The fox looks sad.

'You're crying!' the Little Prince says.

'Yes,' the fox says. 'I'm sad, but I'm happy too. At four
o'clock, every day, I can sit under the tree. I can think of
your yellow hair and your green clothes. You are *my* boy.'

'But you can't see me again,' says the Little Prince.
'I can see you with my heart.'
The Little Prince looks at the fox.
'The red rose is your special rose,' the fox says. 'You love her. Can you see her? Look with your heart.'
'Yes!' the Little Prince says. 'You're right! I can see her!'

CHAPTER 4
A sheep in a box

The Little Prince says goodbye to the fox. He walks through the desert.

Suddenly a train goes by. It doesn't stop. It goes very fast. The Little Prince sees many faces at the train windows. They are all children. The grown-ups are sleeping.

The Little Prince walks on.

A second train goes by. It doesn't stop. The children are looking out of the windows. The grown-ups are sleeping.

'Grown-ups are strange,' the Little Prince thinks. 'They have many roses in their gardens. But they don't see them. They have windows on their trains. But they don't look out of them. They never look with their hearts.'

The Little Prince walks through the desert for many days.

He sees a plane. There is a man next to the plane. The man is sleeping.

'Draw me a sheep,' the Little Prince says to the man.

'What?' the man says and he opens his eyes.

'Please draw me a sheep.'

'Who are you?' the man asks. 'What are you doing here?'

But the Little Prince doesn't answer, so the man draws a sheep.

'That sheep is sad,' the Little Prince says. 'Try again.'

The man draws a second sheep.

'No,' the Little Prince says. 'I want a friendly sheep.'

This time, the man draws a box. 'The sheep is in the box,' he says.

'I can take the sheep to my planet in the box!' the Little Prince says. 'Then the box can be a house for the sheep.'

'Why do you want a sheep?' the man asks.

'It can eat the baobab trees on my planet,' the Little Prince says.

'It's only one sheep,' the man says.

'My planet is very small,' the Little Prince says. 'But do sheep eat roses?'

'Yes,' the man answers.

'Oh!' says the Little Prince. 'I have a rose on my planet.'

'I can draw a rope for the sheep,' the man says.

But now the Little Prince is thinking about his rose. Who is watching her? Who is giving her water?

CHAPTER 5
Home

The man is not happy. He has no water.

'Can we look for some water?' the man asks.

The man and the Little Prince walk through the desert. They walk for three hours. They don't find any water.

'I can't live without water,' the man says.

'The desert is beautiful.'

'But I can't live without water.'

'There *is* water,' says the Little Prince.

'Where?' the man asks.

'Look with your heart,' the Little Prince says.

They walk for many hours.

'Listen,' the Little Prince says. 'I can hear the water. It's singing.'

The man smiles. They find cold water and they drink it. It is beautiful.

'I'm going home,' the Little Prince says.

The man is sad. The Little Prince is his friend.

'My rose is waiting,' says the Little Prince. 'I have the sheep, the box and the rope.'

Suddenly, the man sees a blue light. It's going very fast.

'No!' the man says.

But the Little Prince is waiting for the snake. And now the snake helps him. The snake takes him back to his planet.

The Little Prince goes back to his baobab trees. The Little Prince goes home to his red rose.

THE SOLAR

The Little Prince goes to different planets in this story. One of the planets is Earth. There are eight planets and one sun in our solar system.

The **Solar System** is 4,600,000,000 years old. It's very cold and very dark.

Sun

The **sun** is very big and very hot. The eight planets go round the sun. Earth goes round the sun in 365 days. Never look at the sun!

Mercury   Venus

Earth

Earth is the only planet with people. About 7,000,000,000 people live on Earth.

Mars

Mars is the red planet and it's next to Earth. There is water on it but no people. You can see Mars from Earth.

d) 'What can you buy?'

e) 'Why can't you talk to me?'

5 What do you think? Choose a picture on pages 6–11. Who is in it? What are they saying? What is happening?

CHAPTER 3

Before you read

You can use a dictionary for these activities.

6 Answer the questions.

   a) Is there usually a lot of water in the **desert**?

   b) Who is **special** to you – a person in your family or a person in the street?

   c) Can a person live without a **heart**?

   d) Can people live with **tame** animals?

   e) How many legs does a **snake** have?

7 The Little Prince meets a fox and a snake in Chapter 3. One of them teaches him an important lesson. Which one, do you think?

After you read

8 Answer the questions.

   a) Why doesn't the Little Prince see any people on Earth?

   b) Are people friendly to the snake?

   c) How can the snake help the Little Prince?

   d) The Little Prince sees a garden of red roses. Why isn't he happy?

   e) Who does he meet in the rose garden?

9 Write the words in the sentences.

   four   heart   boy   friends   special   tames   fox

   a) Boys and foxes are not usually … .

   b) At first, the Little Prince is not … to the fox.

   c) The Little Prince … the fox.

d) It takes … days.

e) Then the Little Prince and the … are friends.

f) The Little Prince is the fox's special … .

g) The Little Prince is on Earth but he can see his red rose with his … .

10 What lesson does the fox teach the Little Prince? Choose the correct words *in italics*.

Help / Ask a person and *like / be* their friend. Then you are *special / favourite* to that person.

CHAPTERS 4–5

Before you read

You can use a dictionary for these activities.

11 Match the words to the sentences.

    a) box   **i)** It's long and thin.

    b) rope   **ii)** It's white and has four legs.

    c) sheep   **iii)** You put things in it.

12 Look at the picture at the top of page 22. What is the man doing?

    a) flying   **b)** eating   **c)** drawing

After you read

13 Find the mistakes in these sentences.

    a) The fox goes with the Little Prince into the desert.

    b) Many grown-ups are looking out of the train window.

    c) The Little Prince meets a man with a car in the desert.

    d) The man draws a snake.

    e) The man draws a fox in a box.

    f) The sheep can eat the roses on the Little Prince's planet.

14 Answer the questions.

    a) What does the man want?

b) How do the man and the Little Prince find water?

c) Where does the Little Prince want to go?

d) Who is waiting for the Little Prince?

e) How does he get home?

15 'Grown-ups are strange,' says the Little Prince. Why does he think these grown-ups are strange?

- the king
- the businessman
- the people with the rose garden
- the grown-ups on the train

New Words

What do these words mean?

baobab tree (n) ....

box (n) ....

businessman (n) ....

count (v) ....

desert (n) ....

draw (v) ....

fly (v) ....

grown-up (n) ....

heart (n) ....

plane (n) ....

planet (n) ....

rope (n) ....

special (adj) ....

strange (adj) ....

tame (adj & v) ....

Animal words

fox ....

sheep ....

snake ....